The Reptile Park

Julie Haydon

Chapter 1	The Reptile Park	2
Chapter 2	Lizards	4
Chapter 3	Snakes	8
Chapter 4	Crocodiles	12
Chapter 5	Alligators	14
Chapter 6	Turtles	16
Chapter 7	Other Reptiles	20
Chapter 8	Multiple Choice	22
Glossary and Index		24

Chapter 1 The Reptile Park

I'm Nick. My family owns a reptile park, and I live at the park with my parents.

Reptiles are **cold-blooded** animals that have a backbone. Their skin is covered with scales. Most reptiles lay eggs on land.

There are different kinds of reptiles, such as lizards, snakes, crocodiles, alligators and turtles. Reptiles live all over the world, except in very cold places.

Let me tell you about some of the reptiles at the park.

FACT

In cold weather, reptiles may lie in the sun to get warm. This is called basking.

Chapter 2 Lizards

Most lizards have four legs, a tail, ears and eyelids. Lizards live underground, on the ground, on rocks and in trees. Some lizards even spend time in water.

Lizards can be herbivores (plant eaters), carnivores (animal eaters) or omnivores (plant and animal eaters).

a central bearded dragon

Gecko

There are different kinds of geckos. Some geckos are excellent climbers. They can climb trees, rocks and walls to find food and to escape **predators**. Unlike most lizards, many geckos are **nocturnal**.

FACT
Some geckos can make loud sounds.

a leaf-tail gecko

Frilled Lizard

The frilled lizard has a frill of skin around its neck. To scare away predators, the lizard opens its frill to make itself look bigger. The frilled lizard is a good climber and spends time in trees. It eats insects and other small animals.

Komodo Dragon

The Komodo dragon is the largest lizard. It can grow three metres long. A Komodo dragon has a heavy body and a strong tail that it can use as a weapon. It hunts animals such as wild pigs, deer, birds and other reptiles.

FACT
The Komodo dragon is also called the Komodo monitor.

Chapter 3 Snakes

Snakes have a long, slim body. They do not have legs, ears or eyelids.

All snakes are carnivores, but they kill their **prey** in different ways. **Venomous** snakes make a poison inside their bodies, called venom. When they bite, they inject the venom into their prey. **Constrictors** wrap around their prey to stop it from breathing.

a rattlesnake

Corn Snake

The corn snake is a constrictor. Many farmers are happy to have corn snakes on their farms because corn snakes eat rats and mice, as well as birds. A female corn snake can lay up to 25 eggs at a time.

FACT

How did the corn snake get its name? Corn snakes are often found in farm buildings where corn is stored. The snakes catch the rats and mice that feed on the corn.

Cobra

The cobra has a hood that it spreads when it feels **threatened**. It is a venomous snake and some kinds of cobras can even spray venom. Sprayed venom does not kill, but it can get into an animal's eyes and make the animal go blind.

Anaconda

The anaconda is a huge, heavy constrictor that spends most of its life in water. It often catches animals when they come to drink, and it is so powerful it can catch and eat large animals, such as deer. Anacondas do not lay eggs, but give birth to live young.

FACT

Like other snakes, anacondas cannot chew. They swallow their prey whole.

Chapter 4 Crocodiles

Crocodiles have a wide, flat body that is covered with hard scales. They have four legs, a strong tail and powerful jaws. Crocodiles are carnivores and spend most of their life in water. A crocodile's eyes, ears and nostrils are on top of its head, so it can see, hear and breathe with just the top of its head above the water.

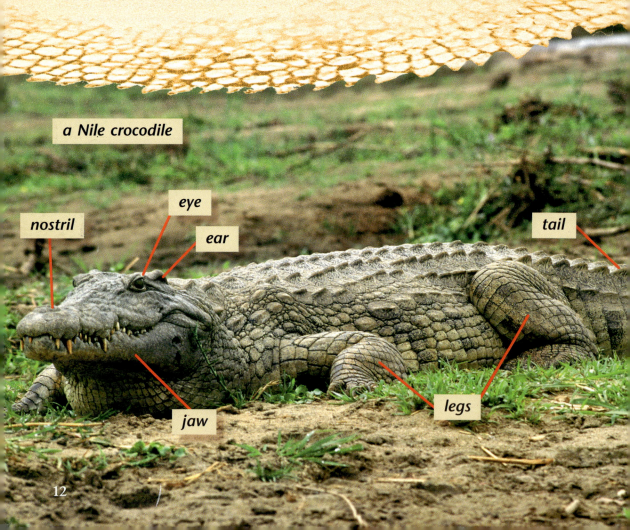

a Nile crocodile

nostril, eye, ear, tail, jaw, legs

Saltwater Crocodile

The saltwater crocodile is the biggest crocodile. It can live in fresh water or in the sea, and it will eat almost any animal it can catch. Saltwater crocodiles **mate** in water, and females lay their eggs in nests on river banks.

FACT
Female saltwater crocodiles guard their eggs and look after their babies for a few weeks after they hatch.

Chapter 5 Alligators

Alligators look a lot like crocodiles, but their **snouts** are shorter and wider. Like crocodiles, alligators can close a flap of skin at the back of the throat. This stops water from going into their lungs when they catch prey. They can also close flaps of skin over their ears and nostrils.

a Chinese alligator

American Alligator

The American alligator is black and it lives in fresh water. If the alligator gets too hot, it rests with its mouth open to help itself cool down. The American alligator can lie so still in water that it looks like a log, which helps it surprise prey.

FACT
Young American alligators have yellow stripes around their bodies.

 Turtles

Turtles have four **limbs** and a shell. Some turtles can pull or tuck their head inside their shell. Turtles can be herbivores, carnivores or omnivores. They have very sharp jaws, but no teeth.

All turtles lay their eggs on land, though some turtles spend most of their lives in water. Some turtles that live on land are called tortoises.

a painted turtle

Green Turtle

The green turtle has flippers and lives in the sea. Green turtles will swim long distances to mate near sandy beaches. After mating, female green turtles go ashore and dig a hole in the sand where they lay their eggs. When the baby turtles hatch, they rush into the water.

FACT
Many green turtle babies are eaten by other animals before they reach the sea.

Box Turtle

There are different kinds of box turtles. A box turtle can pull its head and legs inside its shell, then close the shell like a box. This helps to keep the turtle safe from predators.

Galapagos Tortoise

The Galapagos tortoise can grow more than a metre long and can weigh more than three large men. The Galapagos tortoise is a herbivore that lives on land. Some Galapagos tortoises have lived for more than 100 years.

FACT
The Galapagos tortoise likes to bask in small pools of water and mud.

Chapter 7 Other Reptiles

There are other kinds of reptiles.

Worm-lizards are slender and wormlike with a smooth head. They spend most of their life underground.

Legless lizards look like snakes, but they are lizards that do not have legs.

Tuataras are rare reptiles that live only on a few small islands off New Zealand. They are nocturnal and sometimes share their burrows with birds.

Gharials live in rivers. They have a long, narrow snout that helps them catch fish.

Chapter 8 Multiple Choice

1. Reptiles have:
   a) a backbone
   b) no bones
   c) weak bones

2. Reptiles have:
   a) fur
   b) feathers
   c) scales

3. Most lizards have:
   a) no legs
   b) two legs
   c) four legs

4. Snakes that make venom are:

a) constrictors

b) venomous

c) harmless

5. A crocodile spends most of its life in:

a) trees

b) water

c) the desert

6. A box turtle can pull:

a) its head and legs inside its shell

b) only its head inside its shell

c) no part of its body inside its shell

Answers on page 24.

Glossary

cold-blooded	an animal that cannot make its own body heat but whose body temperature rises and falls with the temperature of its surroundings
constrictors	snakes that wrap around their prey to stop it breathing
limbs	parts of the body like legs and arms
mate	when a male and a female join together to make babies
nocturnal	active at night
predators	animals that catch and eat other animals
prey	an animal that is caught and eaten by another animal
snouts	the nose and jaws of some animals
threatened	feeling that someone or something is going to hurt you
venomous	animals that are able to make venom inside their bodies

Index

American alligator 15
anaconda 11
backbone 2, 22
box turtle 18, 23
cobra 10
corn snake 9

eggs 2, 9, 11, 13, 16, 17
frilled lizard 6
Galapagos tortoise 19
gecko 5
gharials 21
green turtle 17

Komodo dragon 7
legless lizards 20
saltwater crocodile 13
scales 2, 12, 22
tuataras 21
worm-lizards 20

Multiple Choice answers
1a, 2c, 3c, 4b, 5b, 6a